Overcoming Anything

Four Easy Steps to Overcoming Life's Wrecks

Brent Husmann

Overcoming Anything

Four Easy Steps to Overcoming Life's Wrecks

Brent Husmann

All Rights Reserved.

No part of this publication may be reproduced, distributed, or transmitted in any form or by any means, including photocopying, recording, or other electronic or mechanical methods, without the prior written permission from the author, except in the case of brief quotations embodied in book reviews and certain other non-commercial uses permitted by copyright law.

First Printing March 2023

ISBN: 979-8-9877722-0-1

Brent Husmann

brentsbook@yahoo.com

**Brent Husmann is available to speak
at your conference or to your business or school.**

He speaks on a variety of topics and has a unique way of doing so.
Audiences stay entertained while learning the steps of overcoming obstacles.
They will be amazed at his technique for teaching.

Email brentsbook@yahoo.com
for booking information.

"He has been a great student, which he has transferred to be a great teacher."

~ Dr. Jim Wand

A Note from the Author

My name is Brent Husmann. I am from a small town in Iowa. I am not a professional writer. I have a story of my life and my family's and how we have gotten through it. Even though this is a short book, I believe it can help those who are struggling.

Table of Contents

Chapter One 1

Chapter Two 5

Chapter Three...7

Chapter Four 11

Chapter Five 15

Chapter Six..17

Chapter Seven 21

Chapter Eight..23

Chapter One

I was four years old, having gone to the grocery store with my dad to get groceries. My dad was a truck driver, and as we returned to the truck, I began eating some candy I had gotten from the store. My dad asked where I had gotten the candy, and I told him from inside the store. I had taken it without permission or paying for it. He took me back into the store and stood me on the counter, and I had to apologize for stealing the candy. At four years old, I was very embarrassed about having to do this. He then explained why stealing was wrong and why we don't do that—it is a sin and wrong. That was one of the first memorable lessons of my life. There are more.

My dad and I were returning home late at night from getting a load of beef. Truck drivers often hauled in swinging beef that could weigh as much as 250 lbs. apiece. Dad drove a semi, hauling sides of meat hanging from hooks in the trailer. We continued our journey, and I fell asleep in the bunk.

Suddenly, I woke up and thought something was strange, hearing weird noises, but I was still in the bunk of the semi. We weren't moving.

I climbed out of the bunk, and out of the semi, in the pitch black of the night. We had been in a wreck and were down a very deep ditch! I yelled for my dad, and he answered, trapped under the sides of beef. I was a four-year-old boy with shorts and cowboy boots trying to move thousands of pounds of meat off of my dad. He told me to get help. I walked a little way up toward the road but came across a big black hole in the ground, and I feared it.

I went back to my dad. He said to go around it, and it would be okay. And so, I did.

I finally got up to the road and started walking. I went to several farmhouses but couldn't wake anyone up. I was cold and alone and afraid I might not get help. I began walking back to the semi, where my dad was trapped, and a car came by. A lady had stopped and picked me up. I explained to her how my dad was trapped and that we needed help. She drove to where I thought the semi was, going back and forth a few times, but it was too dark to see the wreck. And so we went into town, stopped at a phone booth, and called the sheriff.

Soon after, I was in an ambulance at the scene of our wreck. A lady tried to keep me warm and comfortable. We had a contest to see who would not yawn. She was funny and, looking back on it, was very good at what she did.

My memory of the event comes and goes, and the next thing I remember was being at the hospital with the doctor. He examined me. I had maybe one or two scratches.

Some friends from that small town where the hospital was, were a family Christian singing group who came and picked me up from the hospital.

When my mom finally arrived, I asked her about Daddy. She cried and told me. Daddy went to heaven to be with God. I asked her when he was coming back.

The next few days were a blur, but I remember my mom crying a lot and me telling her it would be okay.

I believe God was watching over me and already had big plans for me someday.

Chapter Two

Growing up without a dad can be tough. I was made fun of because I didn't have a dad. I got into some fights. It is a whole different world without a dad. A friend in fourth grade introduced me to wrestling. I wasn't very good at first, but most kids aren't just starting. The coaches accepted me for who I was and didn't pick on me for not having a dad. So, I kept going and learning.

When I was twelve, my mom remarried, and we moved to another small town in Iowa, about thirty miles away from my home. This meant starting a new school and trying to make new friends.

On the first day of school, a big kid jumped on my back. I turned around and threw him up against the lockers. I thought he wanted to fight, but it turned out he thought I was somebody else. I later found out he was a bully, and by me doing that, the other kids didn't want to pick on me. I settled in fast and made a lot of new friends. I played football, and then wrestling started. A girl, a year older than me, told me I shouldn't go out because I wouldn't be any good. I went undefeated in my seventh and eighth-grade years.

I had and still have the best stepdad a guy could ask for. He was a farmer and worked very hard. He never said too much but led by example. I still wish I could be more like him. We went to church every Sunday and sometimes twice. My stepdad is Catholic, and my mom and I are Methodist, so we often visited both churches.

During my high school years, I continued to wrestle. However, I didn't try very much to get good grades. I loved attending school to see friends, which got me away from home. I would go to school early and run with one of the wrestling coaches who became a big part of my life through high school.

I did start to go out and party on weekends. I never did drugs, but I drank, which some might say was a lot. I still think I was "just being a teenager." I had a broken collar bone and knee and had ankle surgery during the school year. I had a lot of fights with my parents, some of them physical, that I am not proud of today. I moved in with a friend for a good part of my senior year. His parents were very good to me.

My mom was always preaching to me about God this whole time. At that age, I thought, *Who cares? Get off my back*. My mom still preaches to me about God. Today I listen with an open ear.

Chapter Three

I will skip a few years because there isn't much to talk about. From eighteen to about twenty-three, I worked, partied, and gambled. I had some good times and some bad, but it taught me about life.

When I was twenty-four, I met a young lady with two kids who were going through a divorce. I fell in love with her and married her. We have been through a lot together.

This is where the story really begins.

We were the average couple trying to make a living and "live the dream" that a young couple could wish for. Her two children lived with their dad most of the time, and her family had turned against her. We had my family, and they supported us. We were married for just over a year when we had our first child together. He was a fine-looking little boy. He was breech during birth, so they had to do an emergency cesarean. I remember them counting and saying they had never seen that before. I asked what? They said the cord was around his neck five times.

Our son was a bundle of joy. I would get up in the morning and get him ready for daycare, and my wife would pick him up at night.

Our lives changed when he was six months old. Jazz (my wife) bathed him and laid him beside me on the floor. He never wet himself, but he did that day. I told her to come in; we didn't know what was happening. His urine was a reddish, rusty color. My mom was a nurse, so I called her right away. She said to keep an eye on it.

The next day I took him to daycare and told them he had a little blood in his urine. I had just arrived at work, about forty-five minutes from daycare, and Jazz called me saying daycare had called and his diaper was pure red, and she was taking him to the doctor. The doctor treated him as if it was a kidney infection but said he wanted to send him to another doctor. Approximately a week later, we went to a urologist. They had to sedate him to run a scope, and he went limp in Jazz's arms. I don't think Jazz and I will ever forget that feeling. I still believe the doctor knew what was happening and didn't want to tell us. He told us we needed to go to the Children's Hospital at the University of Iowa.

The day before the appointment, we took him to a friend's house, and they did a hands-on healing with him. I wasn't a big believer; however, I had some faith that this might work.

The day came for the appointment. It was Friday the thirteenth. We went to our appointment that morning full of hope. We left that night wondering what we were going to do and how we would get through this. Dalton (our son) had been diagnosed with cancer. They weren't sure what kind of cancer, but they were thinking of a Wilms' kidney tumor. They said it was very common and there wasn't much to worry about.

On the eighteenth of that month, we had the tumor removed along with his kidney. They had to send it to California to see what kind of tumor it was.

We left the hospital on Thanksgiving morning and went to my parents for supper, praying the whole time that our son would be okay.

We got the results back and had to see the head doctor at the University to see how we would treat the cancer. I asked him if I could record it because I knew we would forget. He told us it wasn't a Wilms' tumor but rather a rhabdoid tumor that usually has a twin in the brain. I think he honestly thought Dalton was going to die. He said he had a 13% percent chance of surviving. At that time, there were only 107 cases of it known. Ninety-eight of them had died.

We went through the treatment the doctors insisted upon. They started with radiation, followed by chemo. We had to go to class for about ten hours to learn what we needed to do. At this time, we had all the faith in the world that our son would make it. We asked our minister how to get through this. This was his answer, and I have lived by it since: God will never put anything you can't handle on your shoulders. I think I already lived my life that way, with everything that had gone on.

We went through radiation and a year of chemo. We even had a local news station that wanted to do a story on our son. We had a house fire during this. I was on the road at a food show. The phone rang at four in the morning, my wife Jazz telling me that the house was on fire. I asked her if everybody was okay, and she said yes; the fire department was there, and so was my stepdad, who was going to my parents. I got home that next night and looked everything over. We stayed with my parents for a couple of weeks and found a new house to rent. The actual cause of the fire was never determined. It had started in the bathroom where the furnace was. I had an old church bulletin hanging on a nail with a gold necklace on the nail, also. The necklace had melted off; however, the bulletin with the ten commandments on it did not get burnt.

It was a difficult time in our lives; however, we kept the faith. The nurses would come in and see Dalton during his treatments because he always had a smile. We never thought once that he wasn't going to make it. We were asked all the time how we were handling it. My response always was, "What choice do we have?" and "God will never put anything on our shoulders we can't handle."

Finally, the treatments were finished, and our lives were back to normal.

Chapter Four

We decided to have another baby. This time we had a beautiful little girl. Blonde hair and blue eyes, and I fell in love with my cutie pie at first sight. She was healthy and adorable. We named her Jabezz. We got the name from the Prayer of Jabez. We were a little nervous, wondering if she would get cancer, also. The doctors said Dalton was a special case and not to worry about it.

Dalton was by now four and living just like a typical four-year-old. He loved his little sister.

We stopped at the neighbors one afternoon, and Dalton played with their dog. He climbed up on the picnic table, and the dog followed him knocking him off onto the concrete. Dalton came running over to me, crying. I picked him up and said, "You'll be okay." Then he went limp in my arms, just like when he had been sedated and stopped breathing. Our neighbor said to bring him in and was ready to call 911 when Dalton woke up. Jazz and I thought we should take him to the hospital to have him checked out. He had his first concussion.

A week later, Jazz and I had a wedding to attend. The kids stayed with my parents. We were out in the country where cell phones did not get reception. A little boy came up to me and asked if I was Brent. I said yes, and he told me I had a phone call. I didn't even know the place had a phone. I went to the phone in the hallway, which was a pay phone, and answered it. On the other end, they said it was the sheriff's department, and our son had been in an accident. I asked, "What kind of accident?" They didn't know and didn't even know what hospital he as at

I grabbed Jazz and told our hosts we had to go. We took off towards home, both on our phones trying to get a hold of anyone. No one was answering. We got home and talked to one neighbor who told me incorrectly that it wasn't Dalton in the accident; it was my nephew. I finally got a hold of another neighbor, who told me what had happened. They were on a hay ride and were going around a corner when Dalton fell off his chair and got run over by the wagon. She told us where they had taken him, and off we went. We got to the hospital with a little help from a policeman. My parents were there, and my mom was crying. She had already passed out twice. We told the doctor and nurse that we were the parents. We were made to fill out some papers before they let us see him. The doctor explained Dalton was in a coma and warned us he had a lot of tubes and stuff. We didn't really care what he looked like or how many tubes were in him. We just wanted to see him. We walked in, and he looked at us, said, "Love you, Mom and Dad," and threw up blood into his oxygen mask. They made us leave the room. The Life Flight helicopter was on the way to transport him to the University of Iowa.

A Catholic nun at the hospital prayed with us before we left. We took off for home to get some clothes, dropped Jabezz off at my parents' house, and were leaving when the University called and told us Dalton had arrived and was stable but in intensive care. I told them we would be there in an hour.

We got to the hospital at about one in the morning. We knew our way around and went to the intensive care unit. We stayed in the room with Dalton. The next morning when we awoke, Dalton was already awake. He had broken twenty-seven bones in his face and head. His eyes were swollen shut and black, not black and blue, just black. It looked like he had sunglasses on. We asked him if he hurt anywhere, and he just said his arm hurt. They had over-extended it with the board they put on to keep the intravenous line in. They loosened that up, and he was fine. The doctor came in with a medical device that looked like hooks and pried his eyes open to see if there was damage to the eyes. He told us he couldn't tell if there was damage and explained that we would have to wait.

That was Sunday. By Wednesday, Dalton was jumping off the bed onto the chair. The doctor walked in and said we could go home. When Dalton was diagnosed with cancer, Jazz took a year off work and stayed with him at the hospital every day. She is a very good mom. You might say that it is normal, but we saw a lot of babies that the nurses cared for the whole time. Parents would come for a little bit and go home. I believe that is why Dalton is still with us because we loved him and showed it every day. We showed him we had faith that he was going to make it.

Dalton didn't have any brain damage, they said. It was good he was young because his bones were not as hard as adults, which saved his life. He did have an eye that took a couple of months for the swelling to go down. When it finally did, he could barely see out of it.

We had to put a patch on his good eye for about a year to make his bad eye work. He can now see out of both eyes; however, the one that was swollen for two months doesn't have as good vision.

Through all this, he has always had a great attitude. Once again, I told people, "God will never put anything you can't handle on your shoulders."

Sometimes I questioned why this was happening to us. What did we do to deserve this? I still don't have the answers; however, I keep my faith and trust it is all part of his plan.

Chapter Five

Jabezz has always been healthy. However, she fell down my parents' basement steps and broke her nose when she was about three.

When the kids got a little older, the toys became bigger. Dalton was into four-wheelers and dirt bikes, and Jabezz also liked to ride. One day I was in the garage with Dalton. Jazz and Jabezz were riding a four-wheeler and an old three-wheeler we had. Suddenly, I heard Jabezz screaming. Dalton and I ran over there. She had somehow flipped the three-wheeler. We carried her to the house, and Jazz took her to the hospital. She had broken her foot.

I was working nights, and Dalton was riding a -wheeler when Jazz told me he had gone through a fence. I jumped out of bed. They were getting ready to go to the hospital. He was bleeding from his leg. After we cleaned up the blood, it wasn't as bad as we thought. We put a few butterflies on the deeper cuts, and he was okay.

When Dalton was in seventh grade, we got a call from the school saying he was hurt. We went and got him and took him to the hospital, where they took x-rays of his hand. He had run into a wall in gym class and broke his hand.

That summer, we sent Dalton to a church camp. On the first day, they called and told us he had been in an accident and was hurt. We picked him up and could tell immediately he had broken his wrist. We took him to the hospital, and they confirmed it was broken and he needed surgery. They took him by ambulance to another hospital and had the surgery.

Dalton was a very good wrestler. He had at least three concussions during wrestling. He had stitches on top of his head and was always fighting ringworms.

Once again, I would ask myself, *Why is this happening to us all the time? Was I that bad of a kid, and this is how karma works? Why? Why? Why?*

Dalton graduated from high school. The doctors had said he probably wouldn't make it through his first year of life, and now he was almost nineteen, had broken several school records in wrestling, and had a good job running excavation equipment, that he enjoyed. He has been through more in the short nineteen years than most people will go through their entire life. He is now married and has a son of his own, who was born premature-spent six weeks in the neonatal intensive care unit (NICU). He is doing fine now, at four months old.

Dalton is twenty-four, owns his excavation business, and just had another baby boy.

Chapter Six

As far as my wife and I are concerned, we have had a very good life. I believe it is how you look at things and your faith. Here is another example.

About thirteen years ago, I had a really bad stomach ache. I needed a chronic disease list (CDL) physical anyway, so I went to the doctor. She told me it was more than likely diverticulitis and explained what that was. I watched what I ate for the next ten years, but I would get it more often. I went to the doctor every four to six weeks to get medication for it. It really didn't matter how much I watched what I was eating. It just seemed to be getting worse. So, I finally decided to have surgery. The doctors cut out the bad part of my large intestine. I came out of surgery, joking I was ready for pizza. My biggest fear was having to have a colostomy bag. They had warned me about that before surgery. The first thing I did when I woke up was feel my stomach, and I did not have a bag. I felt great. The surgery was on a Tuesday, and I was home Friday. I felt pretty good after having major surgery. The next Tuesday, I wasn't feeling very well. I hadn't taken any pain pills since surgery, but I did that night. At about three in the morning, I went to the bathroom, and the toilet was full of blood. My mom was working nights as a nurse, so I called her. She said to get to the emergency room. Jazz was getting ready for work by now. I took a shower, and we left for the hospital. I was in a lot of pain, and it was getting worse by the minute. We got to the hospital, and they gave me something like morphine, which took most of the pain away. They did some tests and came in and told me my appendix had ruptured.

I told Jazz they were wrong and to take me to another hospital. My surgeon came in and told me it was not my appendix but where they had sown my intestine together, and it had come apart. It took several hours for surgery. They wanted to put a stint in, but the tear was too big. I woke up with a colostomy bag. I was not very happy. I was in intensive care for seventeen days. I told Jazz one night as a joke to stop by the funeral home and make my arrangements. The nurse overheard me and chewed me out. She explained how sick I was, and they had me on the strongest medicine. My whole body was infected from my intestine rupturing. I lost about forty pounds in that seventeen days. I could not eat or drink anything for a week, not even shaved ice.

I kept a positive attitude and got out of the hospital. I wore the colostomy bag for six months. I had to go to the Mayo Clinic to have it reversed. They did a good job; however, they put an ileostomy bag on me. I told the nurse I would be out in three days, and she just laughed and said I would be there longer. I was out in three days.

I wore the ileostomy bag for another six months. I got so I didn't mind the colostomy bag, but I hated the ileostomy bag. I never did get used to it. I went back to the May Clinic, and they reversed it. No more bags, thank God. I told the nurse I would again be out of there in three days. She said she would see me in four days because that's when she worked again. I never saw her again.

Through all this, we kept a positive attitude and prayed a lot.

I still ask why this happens to us all of the time.

I now have many scars from my surgeries and a hernia. I had five surgeries in fifteen months.

Chapter Seven

After my surgeries, I figured out that life is short and precious. So, I wanted to do more.

We decided to go to Puerto Vallarta, Mexico, with some friends. We were having a good time getting there Saturday, and it was Monday morning. We were talking to my daughter on the video phone. We could tell something was wrong. Finally, she told us she had been sexually assaulted by someone we truly trusted.

She was fifteen, and he was quite a bit older. I'll be honest here; I don't think I have ever wanted to hurt someone so bad in my life. I wanted to fly home, but I knew I would end up in jail if I did.

We got home from our trip and dealt with it. I will not go into this very much because of the people involved.

People didn't believe my daughter about what had happened. It was a tough time for all of us. We lost a lot of close friends and people during this time, all because of one young man's mistake. About six months after this happened, my daughter overdosed on some pills. She thought this would make people believe her side of the story.

We got her the help she needed, and the as for the young man, he admitted to the sexual assault in court and has paid the consequences.

My daughter has graduated high school and is doing well in life.

Chapter Eight

So now I want to tell you about four ways I have learned in my life to overcome these obstacles.

1 – Write down your goals.

I know you hear that all the time, but have you ever done it? Write down how you want to handle a situation or some short- and long-term goals.

Writing goals clears your mind and forces you to focus on important activities instead of just reacting. When you write your goals, you give yourself a destination and daily direction.

2 – Use repetition.

Think about this for a minute. Have you ever heard a commercial and can't get the song out of your head? We have a hardware store in the Midwest called Menards. When my son was about six, we were going into Menards, and he sang their commercial jingle, "Save big money at Menards." He had heard their jingle on television and radio enough times that he knew it without thinking about it. Here are a few more examples:

"Never had it. Never will." – 7-Up

"Like a good neighbor." – State Farm

"They're magically delicious." – Lucky Charms

"Plop plop, fizz fizz." – Alka Seltzer

My favorite is: "Where's the beef?" –Wendys

My point is repetition works.

I suggest writing down something you want to overcome or a goal you want to reach. Make it a few minutes long and use only positive words. Example: smoking. Don't say, "I won't smoke anymore." Instead, say, "I am smoke-free or tobacco-free." Now, take your smartphone or another recording device and say that over and over again into the smartphone.

On the way to and from work, play that recording repeatedly.

When I was in high school, I wrestled. I had missed state every year by just a point or two. When I was a senior, I told myself, "I am going to make it to state no matter what." I told myself that every day all day long. I just kept repeating it in my head. I wrote it down in my notebook. I had no doubt I would make it to state, and I did. The only thing I messed up on was selling myself short. I should have been saying, "I am a state champion."

3 – Self-hypnosis.

Whether you believe it or not, we all do it every day.

A good friend and my mentor, Dr. Jim Wand, and I talked about this one day. He told me what I did in high school for wrestling was a form of self-hypnosis.

I also used self-hypnosis when I had all my surgeries. I used very little pain medication.

From the time my kids were born until probably their age seven, I would sing just a little jingle I made up saying, "Every day in every way we are getting happier and happier, heather and healthier, wealthier and wealthier because we are winners." That is both a form of repetition and self-hypnosis.

There are several good books on self-hypnosis, so I will not go into much detail. I recommend *The Seven Most Effective Methods of Self-Hypnosis* by Dr. Richard Nongard.

4 – Have FAITH.

This is a big one for me. You have to have faith. I don't care if you believe in God, Buddha, or what or who. You have to believe in a higher spirit.

My wife Jazz and I are Christians, and Jazz and I both believe that God is watching over us and helping us get through everything that has happened in our lives.

My point is this. No matter what you go through in life, you must keep a positive attitude and always have faith. Pray! Pray! Pray!

Remember:
God will never put anything you can't handle on your shoulders.

**Brent Husmann is available to speak
at your conference or to your business or school.**

He speaks on a variety of topics and has a unique way of doing so.
Audiences stay entertained while learning the steps of overcoming obstacles.
They will be amazed at his technique for teaching.

Email brentsbook@yahoo.com
for booking information.

"He has been a great student, which he has transferred to be a great teacher."

~ Dr. Jim Wand

www.ingramcontent.com/pod-product-compliance
Lightning Source LLC
Chambersburg PA
CBHW031509040426
42444CB00029B/1264